Damn
Good
Cookie

Damn Good Cookie

poems by Chris Cook

KORREKTIV PRESS

Seattle * New Orleans * Copenhagen

For permissions and ordering information visit:
www.korrektivpress.com

EDITED BY JONATHAN POTTER

BOOK DESIGNED BY THOM CARAWAY

COVER AND AUTHOR PHOTOGRAPHY BY ADRIANA JANOVICH & JOHN GUENTHER

ISBN: 978-0-9831513-2-6

Contents

3

To Don Grant, who made poetry dance.

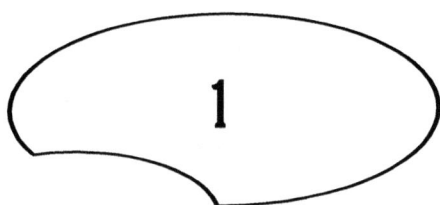

1

Love Down Under

Way up high in the trees in the land they call Oz,
a self-conscious koala with oversized paws
and a body she felt was more chubby than lean,
was obsessed with remaining unseen.

She felt far more at home staying off of the grid
behind thick eucalyptus leaves (that's where she hid);
and she clung there protected from anyone's view,
till a voice right behind her said, "Boo!"

She instinctively tightened her grip on the tree,
then she nervously asked, "Are you talking to me?
You're the first to have noticed me here in this spot."
And he said to her, "How could I not?"

She said, "I am aware how I look—don't be rude.
I'd be out in plain sight if I want to be viewed;
if I want my unlovable shape to be seen,
the result of some mutated gene,

If I want these big Frankenstein paws to be watched,
and this mole on my cheek, and my ears, badly botched—
all these terrible things in one body residing—
don't you think I would not have been hiding?"

In the silence that followed, more potent than words,
interrupted by callings of tropical birds,
he smiled sadly, then said in a voice filled with pain,
"I'm so sorry—please let me explain:

'How could I not' means it wasn't a choice;
'How could I not' gave me cause to rejoice,
and though 'How could I not' had the purest intention,
I guess I should probably mention

I've always believed I'm too small for a male,
I'm too short in the arms and too long in the tail,
and my eyes do not match and my voice is too high;
I've had days when I've wanted to die.

But then you came along and I loved what I saw:
an enchanting koala without any flaws."
Then she looked at him differently, gave him a smile,
and they gently held paws for a while.

Eucalyptus leaves instantly burst with new taste,
and their eyes perceived dewdrops as jewel-encased,
as if suddenly feelings long-dead had awoken
(and nothing more had to be spoken).

They had spent their lives thinking their looks were all wrong,
that the world was a place where they'd never belong;
but they learned they were just as they should've appeared,
because normal is wonderfully weird.

Cockroach Love

Emerging from the rubble, Sidney
fought to comprehend
how he could still be living when
the world had reached its end.

The little cockroach looked around,
then gave his voice a try:
"Is anybody there?" yelled Sidney
(that's Sidney with an "i").

At first he barely heard her as
she gave a weak reply:
"Please help! I'm over here!" called Sydney
(Sydney with a "y").

Girl Sydney said, "I think I'm injured—
can you help? I'm stuck."
Boy Sidney saw her badly broken
leg and gasped, "Oh f~ no!"

Eventually, he eased her out
and made a little splint;
he nourished her with scavenged bits
of chocolate chips and mint.

I wouldn't blame you if you thought
all roaches looked the same
(hey—after all, we've just met two
who even share a name).

To him, however, female Sydney's
glossy outer shell
was somehow more than glossy, so
he told her, "You look swell."

And mesmerized by each of her
two thousand compound eyes,
he thought two thousand grateful thoughts,
and sighed two thousand sighs.

The curve of her antenna made
his inner being smolder:
"O Babe, my inner being's smoldering"
is what he told her.

He said, "We're hard outside to face
the things we're frightened of,
but inside, we are soft, because
we also need to love."

She asked, "Hey, what are you, a poet?"
Answered he, "Not really."
She said, "It's just you're good with words
and sorta touchy-feely."

He later found a box of Twinkies
sheltered from the bomb.
She said, "Dear God, you found us Twinkies?
Nom nom nom!"

They happened on a pool of water
likely not for drinking,
but what's unfit for man, a cockroach
savors without thinking.

Chris Cook

In time, her leg healed up. He joked
it must've been the water,
though she was pretty sure it was
the Twinkies he had brought her.

Whenever they were scared, they lightly
touched antenna tips,
their secret for survival in
the Post-Apocalypse.

Neither could've known that an
unstable isotope
would be the gift that brought their lives
this newfound sense of hope.

They cuddled as they watched a distant
blast that lit the skies;
he said a word of thanks for its
reflection in her eyes.

With hard outsides and soft insides—
that's how they vowed they'd stay—
two little bugs named Sidney lived
to love another day.

Monkey Love

Splat! At first he felt the warmth,
and then he smelled the stink.
In shock, he wiped his furry cheek,
not knowing what to think.

Splat! Hey, what the hell? Again,
it nailed him in the head;
though what it was, was moist and brown,
Eugene was seeing red.

He turned around and saw an impish
female monkey. Then,
she coyly reached behind her ass
to fill her hand again.

At once, he knew that he had better
keep a closer watch
on this beguiling chimpanzee,
this mischievous beyotch.

Game on, he thought, as he beheld
this female of his species,
amazed that she could look so good
while pelting him with feces.

Eugene would be the first to say
his strength was not in wooing;
he'd learned about romance from books,
but not so much from doing.

He knew that throwing poop could be
a sign of deep emotion;
was this her way of showing him
affection and devotion?

Perhaps it's not so much the poop,
as what it symbolized:
something warm from deep within—
a gift, he theorized.

She smiled and slowly came to him
with all defenses down;
her eyes bewitched him, glimmering
like onyx flecked with brown.

He brought his fully loaded hand
from out behind his back,
and shoved it in her face with a
resounding gooey *smack!*

They giggled as he helped her wipe
his crap from off her face,
and then they stopped and fell into
a quiet, long embrace.

She flips you shit. You see it as
a sign from up above;
and she accepts the same from you?
Well that, my friends, is love.

Leonard Grissom

Leonard Grissom had a righteous
funkadelic strut.
He swung his arms, he bobbed his head,
he zigged and zagged his butt.

His friends all ambled sensibly,
but Leonard's groove was rockin'.
They felt a bit embarrassed bein'
seen with Leonard, walkin'.

They said, "Hey Leonard, what's the deal?
How come you always do that?
Don't get us wrong—we're still your friends,
so please don't misconstrue that."

"I'm marchin' to my drummer," Leonard
said. "You hear the beat?
Try listnin' to your soul, and it'll
settle in your feet."

They did their best to try to hear
the source of Leonard's bliss;
they held real still (some closed their eyes),
but all they heard was this: (. . .)

Leonard shook his head and smiled;
he knew they'd tried, but failed.
He strutted off alone again; his
inner drummer wailed!

Chris Cook

It's sad but true: from that point on,
they drifted separate ways—
no longer saw each other much;
sent cards on holidays.

A few years later, word was out
that Leonard Grissom died.
His friends were told. Again, they felt that
silence deep inside.

Though no one truly knew him well,
his friends were pretty shook;
they passed his open casket, stole
a quick, regretful look.

I can't explain what happened next:
how Leonard's friends survived,
and felt his presence stronger than
when Leonard was alive.

The Reverend said, "Dig *deep*, like Leonard!
Celebrate your spirit!
Reveal the drummer in your souls!
Have mercy! Let us hear it!"

And like the Whos in Whoville, when
they joined their hands in song,
it started out real quietly,
and grew 'til it was strong.

The rhythm took ahold of them
as out the church they filed;
they boogied off to live their lives,
and somewhere, Leonard smiled.

The Rebel Lemming

Again, he woke in utter terror,
shaking, bathed in sweat,
as John Q. Lemming had his most
upsetting nightmare yet.

He'd jumped the cliff with all the others,
fell toward Kingdom Come,
then just before he hit, he woke.
And sucked his fuzzy thumb.

A week ago, he rested 'neath
a bush right by the ledge,
and saw a herd of friends and neighbors
flying off the edge.

What shook him was, they stayed completely
silent as they fell.
The vision made him wet himself,
and then he screamed like hell.

And so began the nightmares; he
crawled into bed with Mom.
It happened almost nightly now;
she tried to keep him calm.

Her eyes locked onto his, as mother
rocked him back to sleep;
and this is what she sang to pray
he'd never take the leap:

There's only one you,
And you're cute as can be;
You can do what you want,
You can choose to be free.

That song was what had led him to
a more enlightened way—
a means to overcome his suicidal
DNA.

He learned to be a quiet rebel—
went against the flow;
he idolized Mahatma Gandhi,
MLK, Thoreau.

In fact, Thoreau wrote John Q's mantra:
"Live the life you've dreamed."
Each time he took those words to heart,
his inner rebel beamed.

At last, the day arrived when John
was called to join the herd;
he took his place within their ranks
and didn't say a word.

"We'll start you in the back," they said,
"like everyone that's new;
and don't forget the lemming code:
One does as others do."

You take that code and shove it where
the sun don't shine, he thought.
They all ran toward the deadly cliff;
he reconfirmed his plot.

He'd trail the pack then dart away;
he'd let the others fall.
He couldn't help that no one else
could hear the rebel call.

There's only one you,
And you're cute as can be;
You can do what you want,
You can choose to be free.

He thought of Mom, he thought of Gandhi,
MLK, Thoreau,
then hurled his little body toward
the deadly rocks below.

There's on-ly one you, and you're cute as can be; you can
do what you want, you can choose to be free.

Esthergen

Esther's hormone levels were
completely out of whack.
Her husband asked when dinner was;
she said, "I'll be right back."

She sneaked behind him, cleaver raised
above his balding pate,
then started madly hacking, saying,
"Dinner might be late.

"In fact, I don't know what to make—
feel free to share your thoughts."
And on she slaughtered, diced, and cubed;
she cleaved his liver spots.

She said, "Why, that's a *fine* suggestion,
dear—I'll grill some liver!"
Esther's husband's body gave
a quick post-mortem shiver.

Before she finished up the deed,
she kicked him in the nuts,
and smiled a perky smile at his
eviscerated guts.

She stuffed his parts in Ziploc bags
to help contain the mess,
and shipped him off in little boxes
(no return address).

So now her husband doesn't bother
Esther anymore,
and Esther's feeling ever so much
better than before.

Fluff and Father Murphy

The balls on Father Murphy's dog
were big beyond compare.
He waddled when he walked because
he had no room down there.

The dog, named Fluff, would lick those things
according to his whims;
He nibbled them at Sunday Mass
in rhythm with the hymns.

Confession was distracting, what
with Fluff just lying there,
so diligently nuzzling
his patch of scrotum hair.

A woman came for absolution,
saying, as she sat,
"Forgive me, Father. I have sinned...
God *damn*, those balls are fat!"

Cojones of sufficient weight
can cause some nasty saggin',
so Fluff was forced to tiptoe, to
prevent his 'nads from draggin'.

But Fluff was such a special dog
(his testicles aside);
see, Father had been blind since birth,
and Fluff was Father's guide.

Many were the times that Father
reached to stoke Fluff's head,
and ended up caressing something
large and round instead.

I struggled over whether I
should tell him what it was
that he so gently scratched beneath
that mighty mound of fuzz.

I kept it to myself, and Father
Murphy never knew;
his life was filled with happiness
(and Fluff was happy, too).

The Soup Lady

For years, she ladled soup at school,
all palsied, stooped, and old;
I'm still not sure if she was deaf,
but that's what I was told.

The kids in line were cruel; they mumbled,
"Yuck! Who smells like poop?
It's *her*—the hag." She watched her own
reflection in the soup.

She never once let on if she
had sensed them mocking her;
but certainly she must've known
what little jerks they were.

She had these kindly eyes that seemed
to say, "Here—have some more."
She also had a dripping nose
and weeping elbow sore.

She stirred the thickened surface; globules
mingled with some goop.
"What's that?" they wondered. Someone said,
"I guess it's egg drop soup."

They came with crackers on their trays
(perhaps a dinner roll).
She winked at them, and sniffed...and ladled
up another bowl.

Bulldog Love

"Mom! Look at the ugly dog!" Whenever he heard those words, Winston went to the safe place inside himself. His owner said, "It's okay, buddy—people just don't understand bulldogs." Later, when they passed a store window, Winston thought his reflection looked okay.

We're at that window. Do we see
Our blemishes and scars?
Bulldog love accepts us all
Exactly as we are.

Winston often dreamed of the perfect female. She was bow-legged and had a severe underbite. As she trotted toward him in slow motion, he watched the slobber swinging from her jowls. *Oh God yes,* dreamed Winston. As she passed by, her convoluted sinuses made her snort. *Oh yeah,* thought Winston. He dreamed that her curly little white tail was a swirl of soft vanilla ice cream, and her exposed ass beneath it was the warm, fragrant waffle cone. The pool of saliva on Winston's bed expanded. He woke up hungry for something sweet.

Bulldog love is well aware
We've all got different looks—
That beauty isn't what you see
In magazines and books.

The next day, as Winston was being walked, a young lady came around the corner holding a leash, and on the other end of it was...*holy shit!* She looked exactly like in his dreams! She was bowlegged, had an underbite...why, she even had the ice cream tail! Her owner said, "This is Olivia." Olivia snorted by mistake, and Winston was in love. Their owners talked for quite a while. Winston and Olivia just stared at each other.

A bulldog sees perfection in
The most imperfect things:
An underbite and snort become
The root from which love springs.

Their owners became friends and scheduled many play days for the dogs. Winston was in heaven. Once, Olivia came from the groomer. Winston was indignant that they'd covered her perfect natural scent with cheap perfume. She also had painted toenails and a bow wrapped around her lovely thick neck. Olivia looked embarrassed. Winston made sure she felt especially loved that day.

Bulldog love is wise enough
To know love can't occur
Until we've learned that beauty comes
From what's beneath the fur.

One day, Winston's owner got a phone call that made him look different. Afterwards, he said, "Winston, there's something I need to tell you: Olivia's owner just called to say that she's moving." Everything turned black, and Winston's mind raced toward his safe place. But then he heard shouting... "Winston! Winston! Are you hearing me? She's moving to a place where they don't accept pets, and she's wondering whether it's okay for Olivia to come be a part of our family."

We all have felt the pain of love—
How easily it fails;
And so we share the victory
When bulldog love prevails.

The Reunion

60 years since graduation
little man named Jack
hobbled up the fieldhouse steps
entered through the back.

Found a quiet corner. Watched.
Ancient friends arrived
would this be the last reunion?
Precious few survived.

Went to these for 60 years
she had never shown
prob'ly just not meant to be.
Lived his life alone.

2nd grade when she'd arrived
Jack was nearly 8
teacher said that Kate was new
children said, "Hi Kate."

Never introduced himself
back when they were young
shyness always had its way
paralyzed his tongue.

Must've dozed a little bit
that's what old age does
shook the cobwebs out and froze.
There she was.

He didn't know how long he'd been staring. His mouth was dry, so he headed toward the punchbowl. A short time later, so did she. Knowing that she was so close gave him a thrill that had laid dormant for 60 years, but then he told himself, You old fool—she probably never even knew your name. That was when she approached him, looked directly into his eyes and said, "It's so great to see you, Jack." Everything became everything all at once. He thought he might've been having a stroke, but the blinding lights in his head settled into cool clarity. All the intervening years disappeared. In the light, her eyes were exactly as he'd remembered. Her smile still so big that it wrinkled her nose just the slightest bit. The single dimple in her right cheek. No wedding ring. Why'd he notice that? How would her hand have felt in his? In a slow dance (like the one playing right now), how would it feel to have his other hand resting on the small of her back? He was asking himself questions he'd never had the courage to ask before. He felt new and invigorated. Finally finding his voice, he said, "It's great to see you too, Kate." He was so very happy. This was as good as he imagined life could be. He said, "I'm sorry, but would you please excuse me?" She said, "Oh, of course."

60 years since graduation
little man named Jack
gathered up his hat and coat
hobbled out the back.

Tortoise Time

for Michael Schomburg

The young boy hopped from rock to rock as he happily made his way down to the lakeshore at the start of their family vacation. He was about to step on an especially large stone, when a voice said, "My dear boy, *do* be careful!" The boy asked, "Who said that?" Then an old, bald, scaly head peeked out from within the stone and said, "It is I: Herman de la Mancha." The boy said, "A tortoise!" Herman said, "Yes, well, I suppose I am that, too." The boy said, "We learned about you in school! You can live to be, like, 200 years old! So how old are *you*?" Herman said, "I'm afraid that's something I've not paid attention to." Herman was dignified and chivalrous, regaling the boy with wondrous tales of his adventures and conquests. When the boy was called in for dinner, Herman said, "Do watch your step, boy. My love is near; she's stepped away for just a moment, but she'll be right back...she's lovely, you know." He said it with conviction and a faraway look in his eyes.

Years later, the boy returned as a man, and brought his young daughter and son. It was his weekend to have them. The man led them down to the lake, and was stunned to find Herman still there among the rocks. Herman did not look surprised. The man introduced his children to Herman, who then continued his fanciful stories seemingly from the point they'd left off 20 years earlier. Before the man and his children left, Herman said, "Do watch your step. My love is near; she's stepped away for just a moment, but she'll be right back... she's lovely, you know." The man said, "She's gone again?" Herman said, "No, she's still gone, but one must have faith, boy. She'll be back soon—we've got our whole lives in front of us. And you know, I'll be delighted for you to meet her." The man tried to smile, but he knew that sometimes love doesn't go according to plan.

Many, many years passed. The man was now 80 and in poor health. Something compelled him to return to the lake for the first time in 50 years. He was stooped, frail, and alone. At first, he wasn't sure he had even come to the right place. All the new lake houses with their trendy river rock landscaping had taken the place of the little old cabins that he had remembered from his youth. He hobbled down to the water and said a few private words to the lake because it was the one thing unaffected by time. As he turned to leave, a rock underfoot that looked familiar, suddenly moved. The man gasped in disbelief. "Herman!" Then the rock next to Herman also moved, and a lovely little bald female head peeked out from within it. The old man was overcome with emotion. Herman looked him in the eye and said, "Dear boy...I told you so."

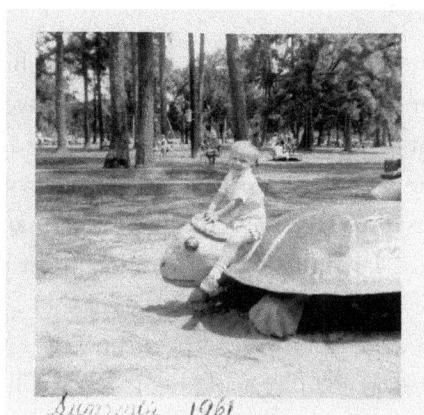

Summer 1961

Oppa Gangnam Stool

for Kay West

Legend has it that they escaped from the school district's storage warehouse and wandered the dark streets of Spokane like 4-legged zombies in search of fulfillment. The warehouse was where school property was sent that was deemed to have outlived its usefulness—a kind of Island of Misfit Toys for blackboards, boxes of chalk, mimeograph machines, film projectors, Eisenhower-era encyclopedia sets, and wooden chairs—lots and lots of wooden chairs. Chairs that still felt perfectly fine and set out to prove it. So they bade farewell to their fellow castaways, broke out, and rumbled about in a weird-looking herd. Of course, if late-night drivers caught them in their headlights, they'd only see innocent chairs sitting by the curb, awaiting a morning pickup by Goodwill. Chairs are fast. How ironic that mankind had made the decision that the chairs were no longer of use, when people are always telling each other, "Hey, you're not getting older, you're getting better."

The chairs eventually made their way downtown and felt the pull of a place called Baby Bar. It was after hours, so the barstools had to let them in. With the black naugahide and chrome of the stools, and the old-school wood and steel of the chairs, they both shared a retro cool. As the chairs entered, they gasped at the uber-hipness of the leopard-print bar surface, the jukebox, the art, the holiday lights, and oh... my...God...the décor was Twin Peaks-themed! Red curtains and lighting, zigzag floor patterns, a white statue, and lots of mirrors. The chairs immediately felt at home here. They were long-time Twin Peaks fans, and felt as cheated by ABC's cancellation of it after only two seasons as anyone. Baby Bar's motif was inspired by the show's dream sequences, where anything was possible, where even murder victim Laura Palmer was brought back to life. Surely this was a safe haven for fully animated bar furniture.

The innocent and slightly awkward school chairs had just encountered the curves-in-all-the-right-places and experienced ways of the cocktail tables. Suddenly, the jukebox kicked on and the chairs stared in wonder as the walls, the furniture, and the fixtures sang along with the tunes, but with slightly altered lyrics.

"Oppa Gangnam Stool!"

Barstools and chairs are smothered by ass all day. You might think that's livin' the dream, but it gets old fast. Only twice in history had anyone asked permission of the barstools to sit. After closing time, barstools are so done dealing with hot human ass that they magically levitate, invert, and cool themselves on the all-knowing, sympathetic surface of the bar. Oh, they ask permission first. The chairs get in on it too, getting up close and personal with the cocktail tables. This never happens while humans are looking—a watched pot never boils. If a person were to run in, everything would return to normal, lights out, jukebox silent, stools and chairs back on the floor. The closest anyone has come is by listening through the outside wall from the parking lot, where they hear faint voices singing twisted lyrics along with the jukebox.

"Stool crazy after all these years..."

Baby bar has always been a world of smoke and mirrors, at

least until the smoke got moved outside, 20 feet from the nearest exit. Maybe it has something to do with reflection, refraction, inversion, or some variation of Alice's adventures through the looking glass. After closing time, the room has at least as much fun as the people at Baby Bar. That night, the furniture did vodka shots (called it "Stoolichnaya"), and it loosened up one of the shy wooden chairs enough so that he started singing right along with the jukebox:

"Are you goin' to Scarborough chair?"

Later, the chairs complained in loud, slurred voices about how the man was always keeping them down, about having been replaced at the schools by newfangled brightly-colored plastic chairs with fancy swiveling desk tops attached to the backs. Whenever the furniture got agitated, the jukebox knew better than to play "Fat-Bottomed Girls" or "Baby Got Much Back," but they loved anything by LL Stool J or Stool Moe Dee, and sometimes even Sonny and Chair.

"Wise men say only stools rush in..."

Even though they sang along with Elvis, their favorite jump-suited icon was Evel Knievel, because he was the first visitor to Baby Bar to have asked a barstool if he could sit, which made him legendary among the furniture. In fact, that night after closing time, the barstool that supported Evel's butt stayed exactly where it was, savoring the memory: the steely coolness of Evel's glutes and the near-perfect impression made by his coccyx, the stool's cushion so sensitive, it knew that the bone hadn't quite knitted properly. Must've been the Caesar's Palace jump, thought the stool, though the chair would argue it was the Wembley Stadium double decker bus jump, and the cocktail table of the opinion it was neither one. They were all hip enough to never speak of the Snake River Canyon fiasco.

Only one other person asked permission of the furniture before sitting. They even allowed the woman to come back one night and take their photographs, the only ones in existence, in gratitude for her kindness. They heard that the photos might be auctioned off at a benefit for a youth art space, and having spent so many happy years serving schoolchildren, the chairs smiled at the thought. As she left that night, the woman heard the jukebox kick on, and she paused for a moment as a distant chorus of drunken voices joined the Talking Heads:

"Stool babies! I'm...an...or-di-na-ry...guy...burning down the house"

The Geisel Revisal

The sun did not shine;
it was too cold to leave,
so they sat in the house
on that dark New Year's Eve.

Dr. Seuss and the Mrs.
just sat there, those two,
thinking, Oh how we wish
we had something to do!

Then he got an idea! A nasty idea!
Dr. Seuss got a wonderful, nasty idea!

He said, "Would you, could you, in the bed?"
"Whatever do you mean?" she said.
"Well, Horton wants to warm his trunk!"
"Theodor! I think you're drunk!"
"I'll take it from HERE, and I'll put it in THERE
(it'll shrink if it's left in this cold winter air)."
"You want to take WHAT and you'll put it in WHERE?
I am NOT in the mood, so you'd better not dare!"
"You see, I think my big thing P
Would love to meet with your Thing V.
And what is my Thing P? You'll see.
You'll love Thing P...I guarantee.
Yes, that's right, Mrs. Seuss:
I've a need for some coose;
I've a need for some coose,
Mrs. Seuss, that is loose!
So I'll stuff your goose,
and I'll RIDE your CABOOSE!

I WILL RIDE YOUR CABOOSE
'TIL THERE'S DR. SEUSS JUICE!"

"*I declare, what is WRONG with you, Theodor Geisel?*
My opinion of you will require a revisal!"
"I'm a lion tamer—we'll hump 'til you roar!"
"*Teddy, STOP! Your thoughts—they're so hardcore!*
You WILL NOT do me as I roar;
I WILL NOT be your carnivore!
We've been through all of this before:
I would not, could not, on the floor.
I could not, would not, in a store.
Not while I snore,
Not 'til I'm sore.
You'll not touch mine,
And I'll not touch yours!
With you, it's always MORE, MORE, MORE!
Well, I heretofore REJECT your spore,
So face the facts: YOU SHALL NOT SCORE–
I WILL NOT HUMP YOU, THEODOR!"

Then something in the air prevailed,
and Mrs. Seuss indeed got nailed.

They made love all day long, like it's never been done,
yet that horny old doctor had only begun.
He said, "Baby, you know I just can't get enough—
I just can't get enough of your nasty stuff!"

So what happened then? Well, in Who-ville they say
that Horton's small trunk grew three sizes that day.
And just how, you might ask, did this all come to be,
when at first, she'd refused him so adamantly?

Well, to those of us gathered, the answer's sublime:
Mrs. Seuss was seduced by the power of *rhyme*.

Dr. Seuss Breaks Free

There were tangerine trees, there were marmalade skies,
I saw cellophane green with my color-blind eyes.
From a distance, the house looked cartoonish and fun,
and its colors were lit by the bright morning sun.
As the camera zoomed in through the outermost wall,
it progressed to a room at the end of the hall.
Dr. Seuss and the Mrs. were lying in bed,
when a nasty idea popped into his head.
He said, "Baby, I know that it works every time:
Dr. Seuss has the pow'r to seduce you with rhyme.
I am Theodor Geisel, I'm Seuss, I am Sam!
Gonna get up inside a your green eggs and ham!
I feel good like James Brown! I'm a sex machine—HEH!"
Mrs. Seuss' response was to simply say, "*Meh.*"
She said, "*Darling, for years, you're the man I've adored;*
please—I don't want to hurt you, but Teddy, I'm bored.
I don't know how it happened, dear Theodor G,
but your rhymes are no longer seductive to me.
Anapestic quadrameter just makes me tired—
and I'm worried that maybe your mojo's expired."
He said, "Baby, don't joke about something like that—
I can make you 'meow' like The Cat in the Hat!
You're as hot and as juicy as Who-ville roast beast...
Do you wanna make love?" She said, "*Not in the least.*"
Though it pained him, he knew what he needed to do:
he would change how he wrote—he would try something new.

He locked himself in his study for a very long time. He neither
ate nor slept. When he finally emerged, he had a list poem
called *137 Reasons Why I Still Love Your Habit of Tucking Your*
Hair behind Your Ear. He had memorized it. #1 was "Because I

get to see it every day." The other 136 were just as heartfelt.

He'd also written her his first haiku:

Beloved Audrey:
forget form, rhyme, and meter...
You are poetry.

He said, "I'm sorry if it's not very good, but I hope you like it anyway." She said, "*Don't.*"

Then he said, "I might slip and go back to my rhymes."
"And *you* can," Audrey said "*any number of times.*
But what matters is that you can choose to be free;
you have proven you can, and you did it for me.
And I think, Dr. Seuss, that that's sexy as hell...
let's go see if your mojo is healthy, as well."
They crawled back into bed, where their passions were stirred, and it all came to be through the love of the word.

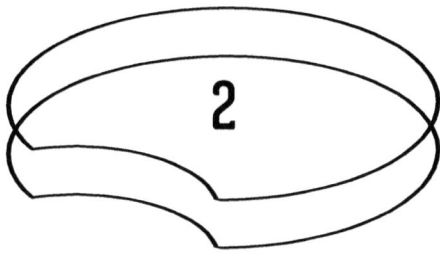

2

Fert

We moved so often that I had come to appreciate those
  who reached out first.
It was the start of 4th grade, and I was the new kid yet again.
It didn't take long for them to start calling me "Cookie,"
like at all my previous schools.
I was told to keep away from a girl they called "Fert".
When I asked why, they said it was because she was gross—
that she had a "bladder problem."
Her real name was Debbie Johnson.
She was tall, blonde, looked a little older than the rest of us,
and she had deep, sad eyes.
On the playground, whenever she got too close,
everyone screamed, "Eww, Fert!"
and ran away.

The only time I was aware of her problem was once
  during class
when she suddenly appeared between our desks.
She was quietly crouched on the floor,
mopping up after herself with some Kleenex.
We briefly locked eyes,
and there was a shame in hers that went on forever.
They also said, "Please don't tell anyone."

Later during recess, we had used waxed paper
on the big metal slide with the two bumps, to make it fast.
I was the first to try it out, and I had the bright idea of going
  down head-first.
Back then, the surfaces of playgrounds were still made of cement.
I hit the first bump going so fast that I went airborne.
The next thing I hit was the pavement, leaving me bloody

and dazed.

I lay there on my back, and when my vision finally cleared,
I found that I was looking up
into the compassionate eyes of Debbie Johnson.
She was the only one who had come to help me.

I paused for a moment.
Then I got up and screamed, "Eww, Fert!"
and ran away.

Friendship

In the library I see a little boy slowly making his way towards
   another boy
who's busy flipping through a bin full of books.
When he gets close enough, the first boy asks, "Do you want
   to be my friend?"
And in that instant, time stops.

I imagine myself pulling the second boy aside, saying,
"Okay, before you answer him, we need to talk.
Do you have any idea who this kid is or what you're getting into?
If you agree to be friends,
where will he be in your moment of greatest need?

"Where will he be in 2 years 5 months and 12 days,
when you get very sick and the doctors can't explain it,
and everyone thinks you might be dying?
Will your friend say, 'You are not alone. I am always here for you.'
Or will he disappear just when you need him the most,
returning only after you miraculously get well again?

"Where will he be in 22 years 1 month and 2 days,
when your marriage blows apart?
Will he say, 'You are not alone. I am always here for you.'
Or will he say, 'Just don't ask me to take sides.'

"How about in 45 years 8 months and one day,
when your mother dies?
Will he say, 'You are not alone. I am always here for you.'
Or will he say it was God's will—
that it's all part of a bigger plan—
that there's a reason for everything."

Because if there's one thing you know,
it's that sometimes there's *no* reason for *anything*.
That sometimes shit just happens.

But you also know that sometimes love just happens.
Goodness just happens.
And even friendship just happens.

You're struck by the vulnerability and bravery of the first boy.
What makes someone so young and fragile
ask a total stranger for friendship?
If he risks his heart by asking this question, and the answer
    comes back "No",
could he ever risk his heart again in friendship or in love?

We're back in real time now.
So the first boy has just asked, "Do you want to be my friend?"

And without pausing, the second boy says, "Okay."

Vibrations

She is always alone.
I see her several times a week, though she has never seen me.
Her progress along the sidewalk is straight,
despite having never used her white cane like the others,
who waggle and tap from side to side.
Instead, she scoots it in front of her,
like a turntable stylus locked into the groove of a vinyl record,
picking up the vibrations of the Earth.
I wonder which album the world has selected for her today,
and whether she likes the music.
I decide that she does, because whenever I see her,
she's smiling.

She never wears dark glasses, either.
I'm grateful for that,
because I can see that her lovely eyes are always directed
slightly to the side and heavenward.
I feel a pang of guilt for watching her.
I was taught that staring is impolite,
but I perversely wonder if it's still rude
if the person you're staring at will never know.
Of course it's still rude—
what the hell is *wrong* with me for even *thinking* something like that?

Today, her path to the store is safe despite all the snow.
The neighbors have kept the sidewalks clear.
It's bitter cold, yet she's wearing a flimsy windbreaker.
Something tells me it's intentional—that her other senses are so keen
that she *enjoys* feeling temperatures in a way that I cannot fathom.
With her bloodhound-like sense of smell,
does she like picking up the scent of those who've passed this way?

Does she enjoy the buzz rush of unspeakably spicy food?
Does she go to outdoor concerts and cozy up to the speaker
  tower to get sent to oblivion?
Can she experience love more deeply than others?
And has anyone loved her?

While she was in the store, the unthinkable has happened:
a plow has passed by and covered her path home
with a tidal wave of brown rime.
The Earth's surface has opened up;
the underworld has disgorged its evil bile for her to try to navigate.
The apocalypse has come.
Ultimately, she discovers that the only way to walk home
is on the shoulder of the busy street that's been narrowed by
  all the snow,
against the flow of traffic.
Ironically, it's foggy and dark,
so all the drivers have been partially blinded.
The cars are going too fast for the ice underfoot.
They have no choice but to pass dangerously close to her.
I know all of this because I, too, am in the line of cars driving
  towards her.
As I approach, I issue a silent prayer and an apology
as my passenger side mirror passes within inches of her.
In that instant, I see that she's still looking
slightly to the side and heavenward,
and that, for the love of sweet screaming Jesus,
she is still smiling.

A little while later, I wonder if maybe I love her.

Elegy to a Hero

Marge answered the phone in the kitchen
and yelled back to the dishwashing room,
"Hey Jay...it's for you!"
But before he took any calls, he always shouted,
"Is it Hollywood?!"
And for the hundredth time, we all laughed.

I was just a kid when I worked with him there at the Coach House.
It was a 24-hour place serving decent food to hookers,
winos, addicts, the deranged, the old, the forgotten—
basically a lot of beautiful people who'd just fallen
through the grate.
Some of them lived upstairs in the Otis Hotel,
or they had come across the street from the old bus depot.

Jay and I worked together in an unventilated dishwashing room
whose heat and humidity would burn your lungs
if you didn't learn to take shallow breaths.
I tried drinking ice water to stave off the heat.
Jay slurped steaming hot coffee all day long.
"It'll cool you off," he said. "You oughta try it."
I thought, "You're crazy, old man."
But eventually, I learned he was right.

He was a great practical joker, but could be serious too.
Sometimes I couldn't tell the difference,
like when I sliced my finger doing prep work,
and Jay said, "Go piss on it!"
"I beg your pardon?"
"Piss on it! It'll clean it out so's it won't get infected."
I said, "You're kidding, right, Jay?"

"I. Am. Serious: Piss on it!"
Later that night at home, I headed to the bathroom to give it a try.
I couldn't tell if the smile he gave me when I told him about it
meant that I fell for his joke,
or if he was just proud that his young understudy
was finally starting to trust him.

The finger never did get infected.

Jay had that pale, gaunt, indoor look about him,
with a tough-old-cuss attitude that said,
"I've seen everything, and I wasn't overly impressed."
He was sinew, bone, and translucent skin
that had been tattooed in his sailor years,
back when sailors were about the only ones who had them.
And he had these impish, sparkling...even kindly eyes.
All that, plus a sense of humility brought about by alcoholism.
Booze was one of the few things
brazen enough to tell Jay, "I can kick your ass."
And then back it up, repeatedly.
I'd seen the aftermath when he was late for work
and Marge would send me up to his room at the Otis to wake him up.
I hated seeing his embarrassment once he recognized me
and realized what he'd done
again.

But he was my underground guru,
and the first adult to treat me as an equal.
I can't tell you how much that meant to me.
He always spoke to me man-to-man,
and so I learned to act like one.
I remember thinking I should thank him for that.
Up to then, I'd never met many people like Jay,

who were hip enough to know that we're in this Earthly
    proposition together—
that it's best to treat each other with enough decency
that there's a good chance it'll get returned the same way.

Ten years later, I saw Marge at the laundromat,
still washing sheets and towels for the Otis,
and helping out at the Coach House when they were
    short-handed.
I asked her if she'd heard anything from Jay.
She paused, then in a different voice,
she told me that the last time Jay fell off the wagon,
he was in New Orleans: Party Central; Good Time USA.
Except that Jay hadn't had a good time there.
She told me that someone had found Jay's body in the gutter
    with his head beaten in.
Marge wept loud and hard as she told me this (she was never
    the type to suffer privately).
I felt bad being aware of the people staring at us,
when what I *should've* been doing
was holding Marge to help absorb some of her convulsive grief.
But I just stood there awkwardly as the numbness washed over me.
I've never known what to do at a time like that.

I keep thinking that since they make so many movies about
    fictional heroes,
maybe they could do one about a real hero like Jay.
Nothing fancy or pretentious—
just honest and true.

So if I ever answer the phone, and someone asks for Jay, I'll remember him shouting, "Is it Hollywood?!"

And I try to imagine the look on his face when I tell him, "Yes it is."

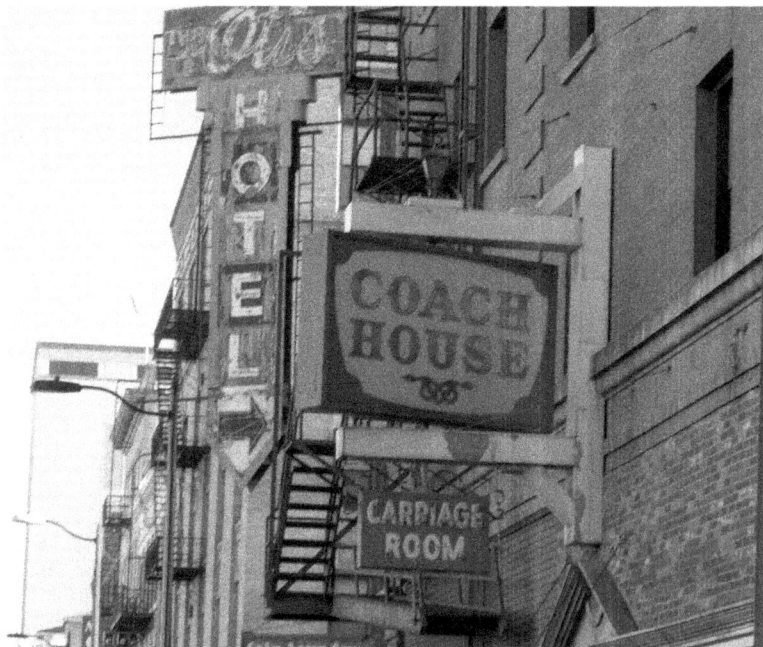

A Death in the Family

for Roger and Ginny Schuyler

I didn't know until after he was gone
that he had written a poem.
Just the one.
It was so perfect that there didn't need to be another one.
It was the one he had written
that asked for my mother's hand in marriage.
On a rocky outcropping overlooking the river
where they would build their home and their life together,
this strong, vital, brave, and outspoken man,
took that poem from his pocket,
unfolded it,
looked into my mom's eyes...

and couldn't read it.

He knew there was no way—
that the truth, and the beauty, and the love,
and the sheer honesty of the words
were too much for him to be able to speak.
Instead, he silently handed it over to her.
And another life was about to be changed
through the simple act of reading a poem.

And now he's gone.

For a while, we were all sucked into the vacuum,
the vast paralyzing emptiness,
caused by his absence.
The emptiness was so absolute, that for a time,

I wondered if I was dying too.
My senses were failing.
I still had eyes, but my vision was dulled.
I had hands, but there was a numbness to my touch.
I was still drawing in breath, but it brought with it no vitality.

I had to find a way out of the abyss.
I had to find life, to find meaning—
to find out if there was anything that still mattered.

One of my first life-affirming acts was to go to Broken Mic
    at Neato Burrito.
Its atmosphere is compatible with life.
There is breathable air.
There is light and warmth.
There is water.
There is food.
It is life-sustaining, it is life-affirming,
and most of all, it is life-giving.

There, we give birth to poems.
They are wondrous creations.
We love them,
we nurture them,
we make them presentable,
and then we send them out into the world
by proclaiming them.

Our poems are love and they are love that has not yet been found;
they are dreams and they are stark reality;
they are clear vision and they are feeling your way around in the dark,
hoping to touch something—*anything*—familiar.
Our poems are sincerity and they are whimsy;

they are hope and they are despair;
they are comfort and they are risk.
Our poems are personal and they are universal;
they are a questioning of faith and they are absolute faith;
they are health and they are frailty;
they are the wonder of new birth...
and they are a death in the family.

And once in a great while, our poems are so perfect, so beautiful,
and the sheer honesty of the words so overwhelming,
that the page must be silently handed over.

Random Whiskey?

for Zaccheus Jackson Nyce

The hobo left the bathroom just
as I was going in;
he held the door for me and grinned
an enigmatic grin.

He'd washed himself, although he han't
done it very well,
cuz he was still a dirty bum
(oh trust me—I can tell).

I went on in and did my business,
turned around to wash,
and saw the filthy sink and counter;
oh...my...gosh.

It looked like grayish powder with
an iridescent crust;
and then it quickly dawned on me:
Oh Jesus! Hobo dust!

Before I knew what I had done,
I'd sneezed and breathed it in;
my clothing turned to tatters, there
was stubble on my chin.

I smelled like double deadly funk
of bathtub gin and cheese,
with just a hint of ass, and rancid
take-out Lebanese.

I'd landed in a railroad yard
so dark I couldn't see;
I tripped and broke my goddamn nose—
you fucking kidding me?

I lost it then; I curled up on
the ground and softly wept.
I'd never spilled so many tears;
eventually, I slept.

I woke and felt my nose to see
if this was just a dream.
The pain took so much breath away,
I couldn't even scream.

A voice said, "Random whiskey?" and
he offered me a drink.
I took the flask, so glad he hadn't
judged me by my stink.

He helped me up and shared his food:
a can of pork and beans.
It's strange how those who give so freely
rarely have the means.

He asked me for a cigarette;
I've never smoked—I swear.
But then he pointed to my pocket.
How did those get there?

We shared my pack of Camel filters,
smoked with no regret.
I drew it deeply in. O lovely,
lovely cigarette.

Damn Good Cookie

His poems were amazing; spoke
of truth and prejudice;
of nature, pride, and living on
the edge of the abyss.

Next day before he left, we shared
his six of PBR.
We toasted life and friends and words
beside that railroad car.

I never knew the stranger's name
(and hadn't thought to ask).
I also never thanked him for
his poetry and flask.

I hiked until I found a restroom,
washed away my mess,
recalling that old saying, what
is next to Godliness.

As I walked out, these two approached:
a father and his child.
The dad said, "Here we are, Zaccheus."
I held the door and smiled.

911

There was a frail, ancient man
in his pajamas staggering across
my neighbor's lawn in broad daylight,
and he was urgently looking at me.

Was this a stroke or a seizure?
Where in the world had he come from?
And why was he smiling? His expression
looked so wrong combined with his spastic movements.

I didn't know it at the time, but this
was one of the most joyous moments of freedom
he'd experienced in years, right up until the
fire truck arrived that I had called.

Turns out his daughter had been about 30
seconds behind him, so he wouldn't have gotten far.
I found out later he had an advanced form of dementia,
and he could no longer care for himself,

so his daughter had recently moved him in with her,
sacrificing her freedom so that he could still have his.
She had kept their new living arrangement discreet,
which explained why I had never seen him before,

even though they lived right across the street.
It was a huge embarrassment to have her careful
balancing act toppled by the spectacle
of the Fire Department and the siren that had summoned

the neighbors, all of whom had come out to stare.
She was so upset as I heard her ask the fireman
why anyone would've called 911. I stood back and
suffered my shame anonymously, which was something

she could no longer do, thanks to me.
The next time I saw him was also
the next time there was an emergency vehicle
in front of their house. He was being put into the back

of an ambulance, and he wasn't moving.
In fact, he was done moving.
19 minutes earlier, he had made an escape of a different kind,
and this time it was to a more lasting freedom.

Years later, the look in his eyes still haunts me.
How was I to know that all I'd seen that day
was the child in him going outside to play
one more time—that his staggered steps were

simply what a very old person looks like when running.
If I'd known that, I might've also known
that when he had looked at me and smiled,
he was just hoping I'd come over to play, too.

Martyrdom

Every year on the feast day of Our Lady of Sorrows,
there's a ceremony for the parents of children who have died.
They're invited to place a photo or keepsake of their child
on a table of remembrance up by the altar.

This year, the theme of the sermon is martyrdom.
Throughout history, martyrs have died in many different ways:
strangulation, starvation, crucifixion.
I learn that if you've endured enough suffering for it to have
   caused death,
you're a martyr, regardless of whether it killed you.

Which means that I'm now in a church filled with living martyrs.
They are weary and bent from the sheer weight of their hearts.
Some of their voices sound choked.
Apparently, these are the strangled martyrs.
I hear a few of them toward the end of the ceremony
when a period of silence is observed,
during which parents are invited to call out the name of their child
from their seats—to offer them up to God.
This is a moment overflowing with hesitation and anguish.

Because what if you say your child's name, and at the exact same time,
another parent says theirs—should you say yours again?
Should you say your child's name again
and again
and again
and again
and again?
Will saying it ten times bring your child closer to home,
back to the bedroom where Mom has washed the sheets

and the pillowcase again, because it's Saturday,
and she *always* makes sure the sheets are fresh on Saturday?

Back at the church, there are so many parents
who cannot bring themselves to say their child's name out loud,
that the silence at the end of the last spoken name
is pregnant with the unspoken names of even more babies.

Afterwards, we are invited to come up
and view the items on the table of remembrance.
Propped up on it are many beautiful family photos from
   happier times,
with personalized frames that read,

"Our Child"..."Love"..."Faith"..."Family"

But off to the side, all by itself,
is a plain piece of copier paper lying flat on the table.
On its left half is a photocopied picture of a gravestone
inscribed with a name and the dates Jan. 1956–Feb. 1966.
On the right half is a more recent gravestone reading,
"God Bless Our Granddaughter."
Her dates span only 3 months.

Losing their 10-year-old child and their 3-month-old grandchild
means that they've suffered enough for it to have caused death
every day since February of 1966.

I imagine that sometimes copier paper is heavier than it looks—
maybe even as heavy as a grieving pair of martyr's hearts.

Later, after all of the framed photos
have been taken back home and kissed

before being gently replaced on the hearth,
a single piece of paper remains on the table at the church.

That evening, the night custodian notices it and picks it up.
Before turning out the lights and locking the door behind him,
he crumples it into a ball
and launches a 3-point shot at the trash can in the corner.

It bounces off the rim and comes to rest on the floor.

How 'bout That Weather?

A first haircut can be pretty dramatic.
Imagine what the last one must be like.

Hospice care has been called in; it probably won't be long now.
Even though you're dying, you still want to look your best.
You can't go to Frank's Barber Shop anymore—
in fact, you can't go anywhere anymore.

So Frank comes to you.
He does this for all of his dying customers.
When he arrives, you prepare for an awkward conversation
(it's happened a lot since the diagnosis).
Maybe like the others, he'll think that what he's supposed to
    talk about is cancer.
Or medication. Or pain levels.
All of which still beat the heck out of "How you doin'?"
because you have no idea how you're doin' anymore.
Apparently, it's no longer up to you.
Maybe the conversation will also include the very helpful,
"Man, I'm so sorry."

But hell no!

Instead, he talks with you about the things you've always talked
    about at the barber shop:
how the Seahawks are doing,
what neither of you will ever understand about women,
how you'd fix Congress,
what you'd do about the Middle East,
the latest bad jokes,
and how 'bout that weather?

Chris Cook

The haircut itself is blessedly normal too.
He says, "How short you want to go with the sideburns?
   Middle of the ear like usual?"
And "Hey, let's clean up the back of that neck—go ahead and
   look down for me."
Bowing your head is something you've had a lot of practice at lately.

You've always known Frank was a good man:
equal parts minister, bartender, psychologist, counselor,
   comedian, friend.
And now you know he's part saint, too.

You're grateful that, as he leaves, he turns to you and says
   the same thing as always:
"Hey—don't do anything I wouldn't do."
And you laugh, but you also realize that something Frank
   would do is die,
because everybody dies.

And a few days later, you do.
As it's happening, your mind blazes through an eternity of
   images and truths,
including something you once heard:
that the human body's hair continues to grow for a while
   after death.
You're gone now, but some part of you still smiles, thinking,
Cool—maybe this means I'll get to see Frank again.

When I Fall In Love

for Norman and Margaret Logan

If there's such a thing as an ordinary 100th birthday celebration, this is not it. And if there's such a thing as an ordinary 100-year-old man, Norm Logan is not him. Because he's keenly aware of what's going on around him, and he's savoring every bit of it. He also commands the room with ease. It's not planned—he just starts talking, and the loud, packed room immediately goes quiet.

He says people ask him what the secret is. Says it's simply living life to the fullest one day at a time. He's speaking from a wheelchair, but he doesn't look like he belongs in it—almost like a guy who's had a long day and just flopped down in the closest thing available. The wheelchair and Norm will never look right together. He's bigger than the chair in every way. Most people look contained in a wheelchair, but he's spread out like he's on a couch, all gangly joints and limbs. It would take a lot to contain Norm, and I'm not sure anything has succeeded yet; maybe the jazz choir that's filing in on either side of him will be the next to try. They are the current version of the same choir he started in 1967, when he taught music here at the University of Idaho. Once they've encircled him like the arms of an old friend wrapping him up in a hug, they begin to sing.

"When I fall in love, it will be forever..."

From their first note, there's a look of utter bliss on Norm's face. There's peace. There's gratitude. There are tears. And even though he's not comfortable in the wheelchair, it's the best seat in the house. Norm's eyesight isn't what it used to be, but his ears are still great. He sings along with the choir when he isn't whipping around in a new direction to find out who just sang that gorgeous one-bar solo, because he's going to praise them for it afterwards.

"...or I'll never fall in love."

His hands are beautifully expressive; they conduct, they applaud, they come together in a prayer of thanksgiving, they wipe away tears, and they suddenly grab onto the armrests of the wheelchair when it gets overwhelming and a man just needs to hold on.

"When I give my heart, it will be completely..."

His face mirrors every emotion expressed in the lyrics. He hasn't just lived through the era of this song—he's actually lived the song. Because of course, Norm and Margaret did fall in love, and it was forever. And even though they've been physically separated for ten years, a faithful Christian man can be patient when he knows that an eternity with his bride awaits him.

"And the moment I can feel that you feel that way too..."

Because he's in near-constant motion, I have to keep shifting to see Norm's face, because I *have* to see Norm's face. The choir members are doing likewise: they're looking him square in the eyes which, given the lyrics, is a beautiful and brave thing to do. Speaking of which, I was wrong about his eyes—they're working just fine. It's just that instead of sending images to him, they're sending images to us. And right now, no words can adequately express what Norm's eyes are conveying.

"...is when I fall in love with you."

When the song ends, he tells us about a bet he made with his doctor, that he'd live to 100. And then this man who'd just won that bet, this man who'd just told us to simply live life to the fullest only one day at a time, said his next goal is 105. We'd be fools to bet against him.

The Trumpet Shall Sound

The human voice came first,
then percussion instruments—
stone striking stone,
stick hitting hollow log.
The amplification of pulse, the rhythm of life.
Wind instruments were next—
breath blown into the hollow tube
of animal horn or conch shell.
The amplification of voice.

These were the ancestors of my trumpet,
which I'm playing for three different celebrations on New
    Year's Eve.

My night starts at the cathedral,
where I'm reminded of the power and glory that the trumpet
    represents;
that it was the instrument of choice for Gabriel and Gideon;
that it brought down Jericho's walls;
that we shall all be changed in an instant,
in the twinkling of an eye, at the last trumpet;
that the trumpet shall sound and the dead shall be raised.
Hey—no pressure.

Having changed from suit to formal tails,
I cross Sprague to The Fox Theatre to perform Beethoven's
    "Symphony #9"
with the Spokane Symphony and Chorale.
The final movement's famous "Ode to Joy" represents
    universal brotherhood.
Its text is from a poem by Schiller:

"Joy, beautiful spark of divinity...
Be embraced, you millions!
This kiss is for the whole world!"
Schiller's poetry and Beethoven's music remain among art's
    crowning achievements.

After ditching my tails for a T-shirt, jeans, and a ball cap,
I cross Monroe and Lincoln to get to Neato.
I'll finish the year playing two Rolling Stones covers with
    The Camaros,
a band that plays music for all the right reasons.
As we near midnight, Mark out-Micks Mick as he sings,
"My heart is bumpin' louder than a big bass drum, alright!...
I said hey, yeah I feel all right now!"
As if on cue, Rob is bumpin' his big bass drum,
I'm sounding the trumpet with my friends,
and life could not be better.

We count down the remaining seconds with the rest of the world.
At midnight, we hear human voices shouting in celebration;
we hear the primitive percussion of pots being hit with
    wooden spoons;
breath is being blown into the hollow tubes of party favor horns.

It's all an ode to joy,
this gift of another year.

A Most Unusual Gift

for Greg Youmans

My friend Greg knitted me this...this *thing* for Christmas one year.
It looked like a swatch of red, green, and white material
with two strings of yarn attached to either side.
When he told me what it was,
I said, "Oh *of course*...a nose warmer!
How...*thoughtful* of you.
This will be so...*useful.*
Thanks a *lot!*

If you knew Greg, you wouldn't have been surprised by any of this.
In fact, he could've told me
it was an eye patch for a Yuletide pirate costume,
a holiday cat toy,
or a festive g-string for a Raggedy Ann doll,
and I would've believed him.

Then I *really* took a look at it,
and I saw that its multi-colored patterns
were artistic and cool;
that it was perfectly conceived and crafted;
that time and care had gone into it.
That it was, in fact, beautiful.

It was designed to be one size fits all—
except maybe if you're Karl Malden from "The Streets of
    San Francisco,"
or that hairy street guy we used to call "The Wolfman,"
the one with the lupine snout,
who walked past Mirage Records every day when I worked there.

On a cold winter day, I remember pointing him out to my
    manager Julie,
because she'd once told me about her aversion to snot and boogers.
The Wolfman was slowly trudging by the front window,
and when he stepped with his left foot,
his pendulous foot-long rope of snot swung right.
You could've watched him for 10 minutes and it wouldn't
    have dripped,
because I watched him for 10 minutes and it didn't drip.
Julie only watched for about half a second before gagging.
The fact that I knew she had brought
a couple of her famous homemade cookies as her snack that day
might've been my motivation for pointing him out to her.
Later, when she handed me the cookies,
explaining that for some reason she'd lost her appetite
and would I mind eating these so they don't go to waste,
I thanked her with as much sincerity as I could muster.

I'm back thanking Greg again,
because I know that I am neither
Karl Malden nor The Wolfman,
so the nosewarmer ought to fit me just fine.

I flash on the fact
that I'm genetically predisposed
to having a cold nose
any time it's 70 degrees or less,
and I wonder how Greg could've known that.

In fact, this may be
one of the most
thoughtful,
meaningful,

and truly perfect gifts
I've ever received.

Thank you, Greg
(and this time, I really mean it).

Goodnight Fred

for Isaac Grambo

"In the great green room,
there was a telephone and a red balloon
and a picture of the cow jumping over the moon."

On the television set,
there was a trolley car and a neighborhood
and a man in a sweater who was very, very good.
There was Daniel Striped Tiger and Lady Elaine
and patiently taking the time to explain.
There was Mr. McFeely with speedy delivery
and how to dress warm when we're freezing and shivery;
and teaching how sneakers are properly laced
and how to make projects with scissors and paste;
and puppets, like Friday XIII, a king
and serious talks about serious things,
like the death of a pet, and disease, and divorce;
explaining the anger, the guilt, the remorse;
how it's not a child's fault and it never will be
(it's so hard when you're 8 and your sister is 3).
He taught us with patience and kindness and love
that despite all the bad, there's a goodness above.
Unlike other adults, he did not condescend
so he spoke to us just as though we were a friend.

First time I saw his earnest style,
his nerdy look, his cheesy smile,
I thought, C'mon, you can't be real—
no one's like this—what's your deal?
But through the years, he proved me wrong

Chris Cook

just bit by bit and song by song.
He sang about us being neighbors and such—
how we're growing inside, how we matter so much—
how it's such a good feeling just being alive...

And then one day he wasn't.

The day that Mr. Rogers died
a shaken planet stopped and cried.

So goodnight, sneakers. Goodnight, sweater.
Goodnight, show that made us better.
Goodnight, trolley. Goodnight, bed.
Goodnight, childhood.
Goodnight, Fred.

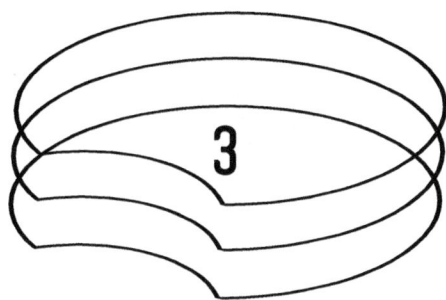

Molokai, 1962

At the Molokai Leper Colony in 1962, Trudy and Cy looked back on the 50 years they'd spent there.

In 1912 in mid-July
Two lepers caught each others' eye;
Young Trudy Mills and Cyrus Nye
Discovered love on Molokai.

She remembered the time he asked if she wanted to try French kissing, and she said, "What if my tongue sloughs off in your mouth?" He laughed and said, "I'm sure we'll be fine." So they kissed, and afterwards he said, "Wow! That was great, wasn't it?" And she answered, "Aaauuuuuung wum bik!" Then she said, "Just kidding."

Cyrus loved telling the story of when he asked for Trudy's hand in marriage. She said that for now, it was still attached, so he'd need to marry all of her.

So Trudy, who was never shy,
And Cyrus, her devoted guy
(Affectionately known as Cy),
Were wed and never said goodbye.

If you asked them independently, they'd agree that the first time they made love, they never actually touched one another. That day, their skin was so fragile, their lesions so fresh, but their love so intense, that they used only their hands to hover over each other's naked bodies, the heat emanating from both palm and body being intimately given and received. They also cloaked each other with the warmth of their breaths.

All lepers ask the question, "Why?"
But silence was their God's reply.
The weak of heart need not apply
When seeking love on Molokai.

He had never seen her cry until the morning he woke up to find her weeping inconsolably. Her left-hand ring finger had sloughed off during the night. She was holding it out to him so he could remove her wedding band from it. Eventually, they saw it as an opportunity to recreate their ring ceremony; they tried her right hand this time. She defiantly said that as long as she had fingers and toes remaining, they would continue celebrating ring ceremonies. The very next day, in a weird coincidence, Cy lost *his* ring finger. This time, they both laughed through their tears.

Later in life, they liked to say that as they lost more of their exteriors, the closer they got to the center of each other. That if, in the end, all that was left of them were their two hearts, that would be enough.

They shared a laugh and had a cry
Did Trudy and her husband Cy;
And even though all things must die,
Their love still lives on Molokai.

Hinky the Clown

He's a local celebrity, man of renown,
Entertainer of children, it's Hinky the Clown!

To book him for birthday parties, you have to go through the janitor at the grade school. Parents find his falsetto voice unsettling, but the children think it's funny.

He's a trustworthy friend to the kids in the town;
"You can tell me your secrets," says Hinky the Clown.

The children adore his balloon animals, even though they only get their choice of a snake or a dachshund with no legs. He always brings along a broken balloon that he tries to blow up. The farting sound makes Hinky laugh louder than anyone else. In fact, it sounds so real that the kids think they might smell something too.

He does magic with scarves stained with red and with brown;
"How the heck did that get there?" laughs Hinky the Clown.

When Hinky's animal balloons pop, the air briefly smells like cheap whiskey. One time, two mothers were talking, and one said, "Maybe it's nothing, but has Hinky has ever looked you in the eye? No? Me neither."

He appears when your bike has a flat or breaks down;
"Boy, it's lucky I saw you," says Hinky the Clown.

Once, he nodded off during a birthday party and started mumbling something about mummified babies. Then he suddenly yelled, "Don't look in the crawl space!"

And he's never content if you're wearing a frown;
"Hey, I know what will please you," says Hinky the Clown.

He uses doll heads for his juggling act. He also teaches the kids magic tricks. Before he leaves, he tells them, "Keep practicing and be good, because remember: Hinky is always watching you!"

Yes, they'll practice his tricks 'til they've gotten them down...
And the children keep learning from Hinky the Clown.

Knackerman

Knackerman cruising down the road,
got hisself a rancid load,
make some room—he comin through—
render roadkill into glue.
Damn, he stink to kingdom come,
make your sense of smell go numb.
Putrid boots and overalls,
cannot believe the stuff he hauls.
They've trained all other knacker guys
to not look roadkill in the eyes,
but Knackerman, he say, *Who care?*
I love to see what isn't there.

In fact, Knackerman look everbody dead or alive square in
the eyes. Anyone stare back, he say, *Whatchu lookin at?*
Better watch out, or The Knackerman could come for you!
Booga booga! say The Knackerman
Booga booga!

Tortured pets long time ago,
kept it all on video.
Sometimes watches just for fun,
feel real fine when he get done.
Knackerman's the misanthrope
who'll turn your tallow into soap.
Smell him comin blocks away,
O Lord have mercy, fuckin A.
Fuckin A, Knackerman.
Fuckin A.

Though children watch, he still proceeds
(it's just like planting nightmare seeds).
He'll tell them, *Hope that you don't mind,*
I've left a little bit behind.
Collects the dead like Frankenstein,
but Knackerman, he sleep just fine.

One night, Knackerman had a dream where all the animals
he'd scooped up had come back to life and found him—
they surrounded him, looked him straight in the eyes,
then tore him to pieces and ate him up, but left a little bit
behind.
Knackerman's body has never been found.

Knackerman, torn limb from limb,
they ate up every part of him
except his eyes, that bloodshot pair,
so he could see what wasn't there.
Goodnight, Knackerman.
Goodnight.

Dinner Date

We're at a restaurant,
just the two of us,
and I read you a new poem.
It's about your fucked-up eyes,
your dry skin,
how I can't even stand
the taste of you anymore.
You laugh, because
you know my poetry so well
that you think this one's about
the baked potato on my plate.
But it's not.

Yenta

Yenta was a creepy skeez;
a creepy skeez was Yenta.
She loved preparing recipes
that called for fresh placenta.

Malcolm

Malcolm has a puffy face;
a puffy face has Malcolm.
He also has a sweaty place
for which he uses talcum.

Will'am

Will'am gots some nasty breath;
some nasty breath has Will'am.
It smell like he *real* close to death...
so maybe we should kill 'im.

Jackson Bluff

Jackson Bluff, a poet, had no difficulty rhyming;
his problem was timing.

Stopped They Must Be

To the poets who awkwardly twist up their words
just to help with completing their rhymes:
you're convinced that it sounds just like Classical verse—
that it harkens to halcyon times.

You say, "Red are the flowers" and "blue is the sky";
you think "Love you I shall" is profound.
If you ask my opinion, I'll tell you the truth:
"MMM! It is too much like Yoda you sound."

Rabbi Larry

He felt the urge to take a piss,
so Rabbi Larry rushed the bris.
'Twas more than foreskin Larry sliced...
Oh, Jesus Christ!

Old Goat

He has stood there since '74,
gladly sucking up trash with a roar.
He's the hungry old nut
with the cast-iron gut;
he's the garbage goat—feed him some more!

Chris Cook

At the First Nude Limerick Slam

I'll assume that we must've been drinking
then the chill in the air caused some shrinking
Oh the man boobs! The guts!
And the cellulite butts!
Oh my God! What the hell were we thinking?

Whammy 5

You've a *je ne sais quoi* that enchants;
how your scent makes my arteries dance!
Whammy sent from above
(come to papa, my love!),
lunch at Dick's: a delicious romance

The Mayfly

At 6:00 one warm September morn,
before the day had fully stretched and yawned,
a wide-eyed little mayfly babe was born
upon an unassuming little pond.
Before he tried his legs, he flapped his wings,
and soon explored the world from up above.
He got to see the most amazing things;
by afternoon, he'd met his one true love.
By evening, though, he'd grown quite short of breath,
and mayflies know that life is never fair;
so, rather than bemoan his early death,
he closed his eyes and said a little prayer:
Lord, thank you for the wonders of this day.
He smiled and then he softly passed away.

Oatmeal Scotchie

Ain't nothin' like a Oatmeal Scotchie,
the treat that makes my face all blotchy;
if anything's as good as nookie,
it's Oatmeal Scotchie: damn good cookie.

Acknowledgements

"Esthergen" previously appeared in *Marry a Monster: Lilac City Fairy Tales 2* (Scablands Books)

"Vibrations" previously appeared in *Railtown Almanac* (Sage Hill Press)

"Elegy to a Hero" previously appeared in *Spokane Shorties*

"Martyrdom" previously appeared in *Railtown Almanac: Prose Edition* (Sage Hill Press)

"The Trumpet Shall Sound" previously appeared in the *Spokesman-Review*

Thank you to Jonathan Potter, for having the vision; to Thom Caraway, for the inspiration, artistry, and energy; for the damn good cookies of Mika, Jayne, and Emily at Batch Bakeshop; to JJ and Shawn at Garageland; to Her Highness, Patty at Baby Bar; to Ted Cook, for the steady diet of good books; to Kathi, for tolerating the demanding permanent houseguest that is poetry; to Kelsey, Melaina, Robbie, and Grant; and to Ginny Schuyler for a lifetime of encouragement and love.

About the Author

Chris Cook's first collection of poetry, *The View from the Broken Mic*, was published in 2012 (Gray Dog Press). Additional work has been published by Sage Hill Press, Scablands Books, and the *Spokesman-Review*. His children's poetry has been published by Little, Brown Books, Meadowbrook Press, and Scholastic Press.

Chris competed in the 2013 and 2014 National Poetry Slam, and was the winner of the Limerick Slam at the 2014 Individual World Poetry Slam.

When not writing, Chris plays trumpet in the Spokane Symphony and teaches music at Gonzaga University. He has toured the U.S. and Europe as a professional yo-yo demonstrator, and was once a nationally ranked foosball player.

www.ingramcontent.com/pod-product-compliance
Lightning Source LLC
Chambersburg PA
CBHW071947100426
42736CB00042B/2297